REBEL GIRLS

Little Library

10+ Women who Help Others

Good Night Stories for Rebel Girls and all other Rebel Girls titles are available for bulk purchase for sale promotions, premiums, fundraising, and educational needs. For details, write to sales@rebelgirls.com.

This is a work of creative nonfiction. It is a collection of heartwarming and thought-provoking stories inspired by the lives and adventures of influential women. It is not an encyclopedic account of the events and accomplishments of their lives.

www.rebelgirls.com

Rebel Girls, Inc.
421 Elm Ave.
Larkspur, CA 94939

Text by Dinah Dunn
Art direction by Giulia Flamini
Graphic design by Kristen Brittain
Graphic design and additional illustrations: Alessandro Raimondo
Portrait illustrations: 4: Claudia Carieri, 8: Paula Rollo,
12: Laylie Frazier, 16: Dalila Rovazzani, 20: Sally Nixon,
24: Sara Bondi, 28: Naki Narh, 32: Noa Denmon,
36: Alice Barberini, 40: Sally Deng

Printed in China, 2023
10 9 8 7 6 5 4 3 2 1
ISBN: 979-8-88964-081-3

FSC
www.fsc.org
MIX
Paper | Supporting responsible forestry
FSC™ C018179

CONTENTS

Corrie ten Boom

Watchmaker

April 15, 1892–April 15, 1983 | The Netherlands

Once upon a time, a girl named Corrie was born above a watch shop in Haarlem, Netherlands. Corrie's grandfather had been a watchmaker. So had her father. When Corrie grew up, she became the first female watchmaker in the Netherlands.

But making watches wasn't the only thing passed down by her family. The ten Booms were Christians who believed in helping anyone in need. So when Jewish people started being mistreated by the German Nazis during World War II, Corrie knew she needed to help.

She joined a group called the Dutch Underground. They helped people being hunted by the Nazis.

Corrie built a secret room behind a fake wall in her bedroom. There, people could hide safely. She also put in a buzzer. If soldiers came to the shop, she would ring the buzzer. The people would quickly hide in the secret room.

One day, someone told the Nazis what Corrie was doing. They came to her house. They could tell she had been helping Jewish people and members of the Dutch Underground. They arrested her and her family. But they couldn't find the secret room, where six people were safely hiding.

Corrie, her sister, and her father were sent to prison. Her father and sister sadly died, but Corrie lived. Her family helped save more than 800 Jewish people.

After the war ended, Corrie traveled the world. She told people her story. She also talked about the power of love and forgiveness. Corrie's strength and bravery will never be forgotten.

SCAN TO HEAR MORE!

Activist and Politician

Born January 1, 1979 | Mexico

Eufrosina didn't want to make tortillas. She didn't want to get married at 12 years old like her sister. She didn't want to have children. But her father said that was all Indigenous women in Mexico were good for. She wanted to be like her teacher, who taught her to dream.

You can leave this house, but don't expect a single cent from me, her father told her. She thought, *If I don't give it a try, no one is going to do it for me*. At 11 years old, Eufrosina left home. She sold chewing gum and fruit on the street. She used the money to pay for school.

Eufrosina taught herself to speak Spanish. After a lot of hard work, she graduated from college. Then she returned to her hometown. She started to teach young Indigenous girls like herself. She wanted them to find the strength to build their own lives too.

One day, she decided to run for mayor of her town. She won many votes, but the men in town stopped the election. *A woman as mayor? No way*, they said.

Eufrosina was upset but she went to work. She started an organization called QUIEGO. It helps Indigenous women fight for their rights. Their symbol is a white lily.

Eufrosina takes a white lily with her wherever she travels. She thinks

Indigenous women are just like the flower. They are beautiful and strong.

A few years later, she became the first Indigenous woman to be elected president of the Oaxacan state congress. When the First Lady of Mexico came to visit, Eufrosina walked arm in arm with her.

Eufrosina showed her father—and the whole world—that there is nothing the strong Indigenous women of Mexico cannot do.

Fartuun Adan and Ilwad Elman

Humanitarians

Fartuun, born February 2, 1969 | Ilwad, born December 22, 1989

Somalia and Canada

Once upon a time, there was a war in Somalia. It lasted for a long time. As it became more dangerous, a woman named Fartuun had to make a decision for her family. Should she go to Canada or try to stay safe in Somalia?

She chose to take her three daughters and run. Her husband stayed behind to fight for peace. They were half a world away when they found out he had been killed. Fartuun and her girls felt like they were drowning in sadness.

Bad news kept coming from their home country. Bombs went off every day. Even young boys were forced to fight in the war. Young girls were forced to marry soldiers.

After many years in Canada, Fartuun decided to do a difficult thing now that her daughters were older. She would return to Somalia to help as many people as she could.

"Mama, don't go!" her daughters pleaded.

"If we just sit somewhere and say, 'I'm safe,' I don't think that's right," Fartuun said. So she went back to continue the work she and her husband had started.

When Fartuun's daughter Ilwad was 19, she decided to join her mother in Somalia. Fartuun begged her to stay where it was safe. But Ilwad said no. She wanted to help too.

Together they work with their group, Elman Peace, named after Fartuun's husband. Elman Peace saves women and girls who are hurt. They also rescue child soldiers. They give kids a place to heal and a chance to go to school.

Not everybody was happy about their work. Some politicians said they were putting themselves in danger. Other people tried to stop them. Once, they even got shut down! But Fartuun, Ilwad, and their team keep Elman Peace going. And they won't stop until Somalia is safe for all children.

Nurse

May 12, 1820–August 13, 1910 | UK

Once upon a time, a baby was born to a wealthy English couple traveling in Italy. They named their daughter after the beautiful city where she was born: Florence.

Florence grew up traveling. Unlike other girls at the time, she went to school. She fell in love with math and science. Her parents hoped she would marry someone smart. But Florence didn't want to get married. She wanted to become a nurse.

Hospitals in the 1850s were often dirty and badly run. People didn't want to go to them, even when they were sick. They were places where people went to die, not get better.

But Florence thought she could make a difference. Her parents didn't like the idea. Still, she studied nursing and became good at it. During the Crimean war, the English government sent her to manage a hospital for injured soldiers. She put together a group of 38 female nurses. They made the trip to Turkey.

When the nurses arrived, they found the hospital was a mess. Hurt soldiers crowded the floors. Almost half of them were dying from their wounds or disease. *This won't do!* thought Florence. She and her team got to work.

They cleaned everything and made sure everyone washed their hands. They cooked healthy food. And the nurses talked with the soldiers and helped them write letters home. After a few months, the hospital became a place where men actually got better.

At night, Florence carried a lamp as she walked around the floors. She would stop at soldiers' beds, giving them hope. Thanks to her, many more soldiers made it home safely. She became known as the "Lady with the Lamp."

Florence wrote a book about what she learned, *Notes on Nursing*. It changed hospitals around the world. Her love of science made hospitals safer for everyone!

Freedom Fighter

Circa 1822–March 10, 1913 | USA

Araminta was born enslaved in Maryland. She was forced to work for a white family on a big farm called a plantation. She made no money and was not allowed to leave. When she was young, she was hit in the head. She was badly injured. She slowly got better. But it made working in the fields even harder.

A few years later, she married a man named John Tubman. That's when she changed her name to Harriet after her mother. Then the family who enslaved her put her up for sale. So Harriet decided to escape.

Harriet hid in the daytime and traveled by night. The stars above helped her find her way north through the darkness. Up north, it was illegal to enslave people. When she made it to Pennsylvania, she realized that for the first time in her life she was free. "I looked at my hands to see if I was the same person now that I was free," she said. "I felt like I was in heaven."

Harriet knew she had to help her family and friends who were still enslaved. Over the next 11 years, she went back south 19 times and rescued many of them. She was never captured.

During the Civil War between the North and South, Harriet wanted to help more enslaved people. She traveled to South Carolina. There she worked as a nurse for Black soldiers. She was also a spy. She would talk with enslaved people to find out information that would help the Northern army.

In 1863, Harriet even joined soldiers in an early morning attack on plantations. They freed hundreds of enslaved people. When the newspapers wrote about Harriet, everyone knew she was a hero!

SCAN TO HEAR MORE!

Malala Yousafzai

Activist

Born July 12, 1997 | Pakistan

Once there was a girl who loved school. Her name was Malala and she lived in Pakistan. One day, a group of men called the Taliban came to her town. They threatened everyone with guns. Soon, they took over and made new rules.

One of the rules was that girls should not go to school. People were afraid of the Taliban. Many decided it was safer to keep their girls at home. Malala's parents allowed her to keep going. But she had to say goodbye to many of her friends. She wasn't sure if they would ever go to school again.

Malala thought this was unfair and spoke out. She wrote about it online. Then she went on TV and said, "The Taliban are closing girls' schools because they don't want women to be powerful."

A short while later, Malala got onto her school bus as usual. Suddenly, two Taliban men stopped the bus and shouted, "Who is Malala?"

When her friends looked at her, the men fired their guns. Malala was shot. Two other girls were injured as well.

Malala woke up 10 days later in a hospital in England. Thousands of children had sent her get-well cards! After a few months, she began to get better.

When Malala got out of the hospital, she had a decision to make. Would she live a quiet life in England? Or would she continue to speak out? It was an easy choice. The Taliban would not silence her.

"Let us pick up our books and our pens. They are the most powerful weapons," she said. "One child, one teacher, one book, and one pen can change the world." Malala became the youngest person ever to receive the Nobel Peace Prize.

SCAN TO HEAR MORE!

Marsha P. Johnson

Activist

August 24, 1945–July 6, 1992 | USA

Doctors had said that Marsha was born a boy. But she knew that was not right. When she was five years old, she put on a dress. Suddenly she felt like herself.

But the bullies at her school didn't like the clothes she wore. Marsha didn't wear another dress until after high school. That's when she moved to New York City.

Marsha didn't know anybody there. New York was loud and scary, filled with honking cars and tall buildings. She didn't have much money, so she had to live on the street.

Marsha made her home on Christopher Street. She renamed herself Marsha P. The "P" stood for "Pay It No Mind." That was what she told herself when people wanted her to be different from who she was.

Soon everybody seemed to know her. She could be seen wearing bright colors, sequins, and glitter. She often had flowers in her hair. But not everyone in New York City accepted transgender people like Marsha, or gay people.

On June 28, 1969, the police came to the Stonewall Inn. This was a local club in Marsha's neighborhood where LGBTQAI+ people gathered. The police tried to arrest people just for being gay. But the people fought back. They turned over cars and set things on fire.

Marsha was in the crowd fighting that day. She was sick of a lifetime of being told she was wrong for being herself. That night, a LGBTQAI+ rights movement was born.

Afterward, Marsha helped start an organization called STAR. It took care of homeless transgender kids. It gave them food, clothes, shelter, and a loving community. Marsha used her big heart to make sure others wouldn't suffer like she had.

SCAN TO HEAR MORE!

Activist

Born October 16, 2006 | Ethiopia and USA

Once upon a time, a girl went from watching the news to making the news.

In Naomi's home, her parents always had the TV on. In 2018, she saw the news of a shooting at a high school in Parkland, Florida. Many kids were killed. Soon after, Naomi watched as young people in schools across the United States took a stand against guns. That's when she decided that she would do more than just watch.

Naomi and her best friend were only in fifth grade, but they wanted to use their voices. They decided to organize a walkout at their school. One day, she and 200 of her classmates got up from their desks and went outside. They stood together in silence to honor victims of gun violence.

What they did that day made the news. The organizer of the March for Our Lives protest in Washington, DC, got in touch with Naomi. They wanted to see if she would talk at the event. It would be in front of a huge crowd of young people who wanted to stop gun violence. She was scared.

"I'd never really seen someone who looked like me—or who was around the same age as me—speak out," she said. "That wasn't something that I did. That was something that those weird guys with suits on the television did."

But Naomi stood up and spoke from her heart. She talked about how the shootings hurt everyone. She also said that sometimes Black girls are forgotten by the news.

Naomi was surprised by the loud cheers from the crowd. The little girl who was so used to watching was now the center of attention.

Troop 6000

Girl Scouts

Formed in 2017 | USA

Giselle Burgess was a single mother with five children. She worked hard to pay for her apartment. But when her landlord sold the building, she couldn't find another home she could afford. Soon, she and her kids had no place to live.

The city of New York put them in a shelter with other families. While there, Giselle was working at the Girl Scouts of Greater New York. She thought, *Why not start a troop in the shelter?* So she did.

At the first meeting, there were just eight girls. Three of them were Giselle's own daughters. She wasn't sure if the troop would work. But then she spread the word. Eventually, the troop grew. They had more than

600 members in 20 shelters. Giselle was so proud!

Giselle loves how the girls in the troop support each other through hard times. "If one gives up," she says, "not too far behind are two other ones that say, 'Yes you can, you can do it.'"

Giselle's daughter Karina agrees. She says, "We're like a pack. If one of us is down, the rest of us will be there to pick them back up." Before the troop, Karina didn't know many other girls in the shelter. But now they all look forward to seeing each other.

Like other Girl Scouts and Girl Guides, Karina and her friends love adventure. They sell cookies so they have money for trips, crafts, and Girl Scout camp. One year they sold 30,000 boxes of cookies in one week—pretty sweet!

Xiye Bastida

Activist

Born April 18, 2002 | Mexico and USA

Once upon a time, there was a girl whose name meant "soft rain." But in Xiye's hometown in Mexico, it had not rained in years. The lake dried up. Crops died. After two years, the rain finally came—but it wasn't a normal storm. It poured and poured until the land flooded.

When Xiye was 15, she and her family had to move to New York City. There she saw the damage left by Hurricane Sandy. The huge storm made it clear that the climate was in crisis. She had to do something to make it right. She began working with her school's environmental club.

Xiye's Indigenous people, the Otomi-Toltec, understood it was important to live in balance with the environment. “We take care of the Earth because the Earth takes care of us,” she was taught. Something was wrong with the Earth, and Xiye was ready to help.

A few years later, Xiye organized a strike at her school in New York. She led 600 students to walk out of class. They demanded that governments take action to stop climate change and protect the planet.

Months later, Xiye and other young activists led a week of strikes. They fought to stop climate change and support Indigenous rights. It took a lot of time and effort. Xiye had to give up gymnastics and other activities she loved. But she knew the Earth was worth it.

"Indigenous people have been taking care of the Earth for thousands of years because that is their culture," Xiye said. But this work is not a hobby. She said, "It's a way of life."

SCAN TO HEAR MORE!

About Rebel Girls

Rebel Girls is a global, multi-platform empowerment brand dedicated to helping raise the most inspired and confident generation of girls through content, experiences, products, and community. Originating from an international best-selling children's book, Rebel Girls amplifies stories of real-life women throughout history, geography, and field of excellence. With a growing community of nearly 20 million self-identified Rebel Girls spanning more than 100 countries, the brand engages with Generation Alpha through its book series, award-winning podcast, events, and merchandise. With the 2021 launch of the Rebel Girls app, the company has created a flagship destination for girls to explore a wondrous world filled with inspiring true stories of extraordinary women.

As a B Corp, we're part of a global community of businesses that meet high standards of social and environmental impact.

Join the Rebel Girls community:

Facebook: facebook.com/rebelgirls
Instagram: @rebelgirls
Twitter: @rebelgirlsbook
TikTok: @rebelgirlsbook
Web: rebelgirls.com
Podcast: rebelgirls.com/podcast
App: rebelgirls.com/audio

If you liked this book, please take a moment to review it wherever you prefer!